S0-ARO-146

BALSAMIC VINEGAR
OF MODENA

ROSSINI

Aceto
Balsamico
di Modena

Product of Italy

500 ml   6%

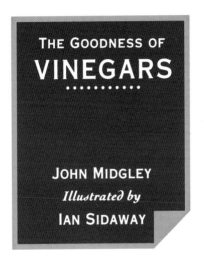

THE GOODNESS OF
VINEGARS

JOHN MIDGLEY

Illustrated by

IAN SIDAWAY

RANDOM HOUSE
NEW YORK

ACKNOWLEDGEMENTS

The author thanks Sue Midgley and Jo Swinnerton
for kindly checking the text.

FURTHER READING

Food in History, by Reay Tannahill (Penguin);
For those interested in reading more about food and health
The American Heart Association Cookbook, Fifth Edition
(Random House) and *Superfoods* by Michael Van Straten and
Barbara Griggs (Dorling Kindersley) are recommended.

Copyright © 1994 by John Midgley
Illustrations copyright © 1994 by Ian Sidaway
Conceived and designed by Andrew Barron and John Midgley

All rights reserved under the International and Pan-American
Copyright Conventions.

Published in the United States by Random House, Inc., New York.

This work was published in the United Kingdom by
Pavilion Books Limited, London.

ISBN 0-679-43360-0

Library of Congress Cataloging-in-Publication Data
Midgley, John.
The goodness of vinegars/John Midgley: illustrated by Ian Sidaway.
p. cm. — (The Goodness of)
ISBN 0-679-43360-0
1. Cookery (Vinegar) 2. Vinegar. I. Title. II. Series:
Midgley, John. Goodness of.
TX819. V5M53 1994
641.6'22 — dc20   93-48529

Manufactured in Hong Kong

2 4 6 8 9 7 5 3

First U.S. Edition

Contents
. . . .

PART ONE

VINEGAR

W ine vinegar is almost certainly as old as wine itself, and rice vinegar probably dates back to the first rice wine. Like olive oil, vinegar is both ancient and fashionable, and increasingly prominent in contemporary kitchens.

The Shorter Oxford English Dictionary defines vinegar as 'a liquid (consisting of acetic acid in a dilute form) produced by the acetous fermentation of wine and some other alcoholic liquors or special compounds, and employed in the preparation of food (or as a relish to this)'.

Wine vinegar is the most familiar, and our English word ultimately derives from the Latin *vinum acrum,* via the medieval French word *vin-aigre,* which mean 'sour wine'. Spain and Italy make exquisite vinegars from sherry and aged unfortified wines, while France has impressive aged red wine vinegars as well as fine white wine vinegars made by traditional slow fermentation; champagne vinegar is perhaps the best white wine vinegar.

Various herbs and fruits such as tarragon, thyme, mint, garlic, lemons and raspberries are commonly added to white wine vinegar for flavour. Flavoured vinegars are readily available or, better still, they may be easily created at home, at relatively little expense (recipes are included in this book).

True balsamic vinegar – *aceto balsamico tradizionale* – made in and around the northern Italian town of Modena is undoubtedly the most aristocratic vinegar. For centuries this has been made privately on individual estates and farmsteads, and some very rare balsamic vinegars are over a hundred years old. Commercially made balsamic vinegar, labelled with the suffix *di Modena* is an inferior though excellent and affordable substitute.

Vinegars are also made with other fruit and grains. In temperate climates, for example, cider vinegar (from apples), malt vinegar and distilled malt vinegar (from barley), and spirit vinegar (a distilled product of molasses or sugar beet alcohol) are common. Asian countries such as China and Japan produce rice vinegars (which may or may not be distilled), as well as other vinegars made from sorghum, millet and wheat.

Wine vinegar

Wine vinegar is a liquid containing 5–7% acetic acid. Acetic acid is produced by a second fermentation, when the bacterium Acetobacter acts upon wine. Although this does occur naturally when wine is left out in the sun, most wine vinegar is 'manufactured' in large vats called acetators, under controlled conditions and with the aid of cultivated strains of the bacterium. Quality varies according to the wines used, the temperature and the duration of acetic fermentation. Vinegar fermented in a modern acetator at 30°C/86°F is quicker to make and therefore cheaper to produce than vinegar made by the traditional slow Orléans method, according to which wine is allowed to ferment at a lower temperature (about 21°C/70°F) in traditional wooden vats rather than in acetators.

Once acetified, wine vinegar is stored prior to filtering, and the duration varies from a few weeks to many months. Aged red wine vinegar, for example, may be matured in wood for over six months. Then it is diluted down to the required level of acetic acid, and finally bottled. Most vinegars are pasteurized prior to bottling. Other vinegars from fine wines include champagne vinegar, Bordeaux vinegar, Rioja vinegar, and some newer California vinegars made from zinfandel and other grape varieties. Fine vinegars smell pleasantly rounded, not too sharp and sour.

Flavoured wine vinegars

Vinegars – mostly made from white wine – that have been flavoured with herbs, spices, fruits and vegetables are commonly available in delicatessens and specialist food shops. The best are made with fresh ingredients. More often, however, natural lemon, raspberry or strawberry essences are used instead. Flavoured vinegars were especially popular at the turn of the century. Spiced vinegar is particularly useful for anyone contemplating making pickles and preserves at home.

Sherry vinegar

Although technically a wine vinegar, sherry vinegar deserves a special mention. Sherry – *oloroso* sherry or the drier, spicier *fino* – is made by the *solera* system. This is essentially a blending process, which permits the continual replenishment of the entire spectrum of ageing wines stored in the *bodega* or sherry warehouse, from young to very old. It allows the producer to maintain continuity of supply and consistency of quality. In some cases, traces of wines a century old co-exist in the bottle with a whole range of progressively younger wines. Sherry vinegar is also made by the *solera* system. Casks of blended sherry are converted into fine vinegar by *Acetobacter*. These vinegars are rich, full-flavoured yet mellow, and may cost as much as sherry.

Balsamic vinegar

This inky, sweet and subtle vinegar is fast growing in popularity in Britain and North America, making it a very fashionable ingredient.

The traditional kind is virtually unobtainable, since it is invariably reserved for private consumption or sold only in minute quantities. Commercial balsamic vinegar – the kind that we can buy – is produced in and around the town of Modena, in the Emilia-Romagna region of Italy. Production began in the mid-1960s, allowing much cheaper vinegars to be marketed internationally as *aceto balsamico di Modena*. It is made with aged wine which is acetified under controlled conditions, and which may also be flavoured with caramel or boiled grape must (the pressed grapes ready for fermentation), predominantly from Trebbiano grapes. The vinegar is then matured in wooden barrels for several years before bottling. The longer the maturation, the better the quality.

The traditional method, however, produces a far superior vinegar. Grape juice is boiled down to a dense, rich must, which is then very slowly fermented in casks treated with *Acetobacter*. The vinegar very gradually develops an amazing complexity by absorbing the character of several different wooden casks, fashioned from oak, ash, cherry, sweet chestnut, mulberry and juniper. Some families mature their vinegar for 15 or even 20 years. Traditionally, vinegars of different ages are blended together, and, like sherry vinegar, some samples of *aceto tradizionale* may contain traces of centennial vinegar.

Cider vinegar

Cider vinegar is made wherever apples are grown for the table and for cider. It is sweeter and slightly less acid than wine vinegar, and the best kind tastes and smells distinctively of apples. It can be fermented into an alcoholic liquid from apple juice or pulp and then acetified or acetified from cider. Cider vinegar is usually reserved for pickling and preserves. Its colour varies from pale to rich gold, and may sometimes appear slightly cloudy; this does not imply deterioration.

Malt vinegar

It is often said that malt vinegar tastes just as you would expect ale to taste if left out for a while to sour naturally. This is only partly accurate, because although, like beer, malt vinegar is made from malted barley, it lacks the hops that help to flavour beer.

First, the grain is heated to release a liquid called the wort. Then yeast is added to ferment the wort, converting its sugars into alcohol. This liquor is fermented a second time to turn the alcohol into acetic acid, either in vats treated with *Acetobacter* or in an acetator. The vinegar is then stored before filtration and bottling.

A darker malt vinegar is produced by the addition of caramel, and if the product is distilled, the result is a stronger colourless vinegar which is mainly used in pickling.

Rice vinegar

Rice vinegar is made in much the same way as other vinegars, either from fermented rice or from rice wine, and it varies considerably in acidity, sweetness and strength. Chinese rice vinegars are usually stronger than clear or light Japanese ones, which are generally mild and mellow. Chinese rice vinegars may be clear, red or the colour of soy sauce.

The Goodness of Vinegar
··········

Although vinegar and pepper were prescribed by Hippocrates to treat respiratory diseases and infections of the lungs – a sound practice, since sharp, 'hot' substances act as expectorants – vinegar's main virtue is indirect, as a natural food preservative. Since the Middle Ages, vinegar has been used to preserve fresh fruit and vegetables, and manufacturers of quality preserves still prefer vinegar to alternative artificial preservatives. These substances can be harmful to certain individuals and today's discriminating, health-conscious consumers are rejecting foods treated with unwanted artificial additives and preservatives.

Vinegar preserves by destroying the micro-organisms that cause food to spoil and decay. Like garlic, vinegar has strong antibacterial properties, and may even be beneficial in the diet, in much the same way as garlic. Balsamic vinegar may have been used originally as a therapeutic balm (see the next section), but its name is more likely to allude to the mellow, soothing aroma of the very best aged balsamic vinegar.

In China, rice was first fermented into wine several thousands of years ago; rice wine certainly existed *c*. 600 BC. It is likely that the Chinese – like the Greeks and Romans and their wine vinegar – used as a condiment rice wine naturally soured by wild *Acetobacter*.

Around the time of the Moorish invasion of Spain, the Islamic caliphs of Baghdad imported vast amounts of vinegar and vinegary sauces for their sophisticated kitchens, appreciating their depth and sourness. Vinegar was an acceptable alternative to wine, which was proscribed.

Vinegar was widely used as a preservative during the Middle Ages, allowing the storage of pickled and conserved fruits and vegetables for consumption in the harsh, lean months of winter and early spring, when, together with a few winter crops and easily stored vegetables such as onions and garlic, they provided virtually the only source of vitamins. Great medieval and Renaissance chefs such as Taillevent and Scappi valued vinegar and verjuice (made from sour fruits) as sharp, appetizing flavourings.

For centuries balsamic vinegar has been treasured in Emilia-Romagna. It may originally have been used medicinally, since 'balsam' is synonymous with 'balm', defined *inter alia* as 'an aromatic ointment used for soothing pain or healing wounds'. Later, it was inhaled for pleasure, like perfume, and also drunk as a digestive.

The Victorians and Edwardians used all manner of flavoured vinegars; my Edwardian edition of *Mrs Beeton's Book of Household Management* gives 17 recipes for vinegars, flavoured with a host of ingredients, including celery and tomatoes. The evolution of a colonial Anglo-Indian cuisine helped to make exotic fruit pickles, chutneys and vinegary conserves popular. Today balsamic vinegar, sherry vinegar and flavoured vinegars in particular enjoy a renewed popularity that has elevated them in fashionable kitchens on both sides of the Atlantic. (Meanwhile, the time-honoured British habit of dousing fish and chips with malt vinegar shows no sign of decline.) At the same time, an explosion of interest in Asian cuisines has allowed a growing number of people to sample the rice vinegars of the Far East.

The best wine vinegars are astonishingly costly, reflecting the quality of the wine and the high costs of manufacture. These costs are inevitable because of the traditional slow methods of fermentation, acetation and maturation. However, the price is well worth paying, since only very small amounts of aged wine, champagne, sherry or balsamic vinegars will totally transform a dish. In salads dressed with the best mellow vinegars, oil may be omitted altogether. As a very general rule of thumb, the more you pay, the better the quality. A pleasant complex smell is a reliable indication of a vinegar's pedigree.

For pickling and preserving, cheaper vinegars are recommended. White wine vinegar or cider vinegar are good choices, although malt vinegar and distilled malt vinegar are often preferred; the latter, being stronger, is more effective with watery vegetables.

Flavoured vinegars are all the rage. Their purpose is to add interest to salads, marinades, pickles and preserves. Besides being fun to make, they look good, smell wonderful, and allow experimentation with an interesting range of flavours. White wine vinegar is the best choice, and in addition to the recipes provided in this book, the cook may choose to try out other flavourings such as ginger, lemon grass, edible flowers, wild blackberries, lemon, honey, peppercorns, and chilies, to name but a few. The possibilities for interesting marriages of perfume and flavour are almost endless.

Vinegars are indispensable in other ways. Many classic sauces such as mayonnaise, hollandaise, Béarnaise and *sauce rémoulade* depend upon wine vinegar. Vinaigrettes also are made with wine vinegar, but more exotic versions may include rice vinegar. Vinegar seems to have an affinity with hot, spicy

foods and tomato sauces. Rich, mellow vinegars make very good sauces and gravies, and go well with hearty braised or casseroled meat dishes. Balsamic vinegar is equally delicious added to poultry or meat, and it even complements fresh fruits such as strawberries. Marcella Hazan recommends slicing strawberries, then macerating them in sugar for 30 minutes, and finally adding a little balsamic vinegar just before serving; I have tried this Italian recipe and can vouch that it is delicious.

Vinegars should be always be stored in a cool place, preferably somewhere dark and definitely out of strong direct light; they should keep almost indefinitely.

PART TWO

· · · · · · · · · ·

Herbal Vinegars

Herbal vinegars are very easy to make and can be used to flavour salads, marinades, stews and sauces. White wine vinegar is the best base, and use only sterilized bottles, sealing with clean corks or plastic-lined bottle tops. (Scrupulously clean equipment can be sterilized by a few minutes' immersion in freshly boiled water.) Bottles of herbal vinegars make especially attractive gifts.

Tarragon vinegar

Wash some sprigs of fresh French tarragon and pat them dry with kitchen paper (paper towel). Put them into a 560ml/1 pint glass bottle. Heat the same volume of white wine vinegar without boiling. Pour into the bottle to cover the tarragon. Allow the liquid to cool before screwing on the lid or stopping with a clean cork. Leave to infuse for 1 week.

Rosemary vinegar

Proceed as above, substituting sprigs of rosemary.

Mint vinegar

Wash enough fresh spearmint to fill a teacup, discarding any stalks. Pat dry and stuff the leaves into a 560ml/1 pint bottle. Heat the vinegar without boiling. Pour it into the bottle to cover the mint. Allow to cool before sealing, leave to infuse for 1 week then strain into a fresh bottle.

FRUIT VINEGARS

· · · · · · · · · ·

Soft fruits and berries such as cherries, strawberries and raspberries make wonderful red or pink scented vinegars. They were very popular at the turn of the century, then enjoyed a renaissance in the 1970s, riding the wave of *nouvelle cuisine*. They are exceptionally easy to prepare, requiring only fresh fruit, good white wine vinegar and sterilized glass containers (clean vinegar bottles with plastic-lined screw tops are ideal). They make attractive gourmet gifts, and can be used to flavour marinades and salads or in desserts instead of lemon juice.

225g/8oz cherries, raspberries or strawberries, washed
560ml/1 pint/2 cups white wine vinegar

Stone (pit) the cherries, if using, but leave the berries whole. Warm the vinegar in an enamelled pan, then pour it into a sterilized jar or bowl big enough to accommodate the fruit. Add the fruit, cover and leave in a warm place for one week to draw out flavour and colour. Shake the container periodically.

Have ready a clean glass bottle. Strain the vinegar into it, discarding the fruit. Seal with a clean, plastic-lined stopper or with a cork that you have sterilized in boiling water. Store in a cool, dark place.

GARLIC VINEGAR

T his produces a very powerful and aromatic vinegar, suitable for adding to marinades and for flavouring robust stews and sauces. This will fill a 500ml/15fl oz bottle.

1 whole head of garlic
450ml/³⁄₄ pint/1¹⁄₂ cups red wine vinegar

Separate the garlic cloves but do not bother to peel them. If you like, tap each clove lightly with a mallet just to loosen the skins. Put the cloves into a clean glass bottle (you will have to do this one by one, and the fatter cloves may need to be pushed down the neck with a skewer). Warm the vinegar without boiling. Carefully pour it into the bottle. Seal with a clean cork or with a plastic-lined screw top lid. Store somewhere cool and dark for at least 3 weeks before using very sparingly.

The classic vinaigrette or 'French dressing' is an emulsified mixture of oil, wine vinegar, salt and pepper; sometimes, however, mustard, a crushed garlic clove or some chopped fresh herbs are added. The Italians, Spaniards and Greeks, on the other hand, do not generally bother to emulsify the ingredients, preferring simply to pour oil and vinegar over lightly salted salad leaves. The following recipes make enough vinaigrette to dress a salad serving four people.

Classic vinaigrette

3–4 tbs refined olive oil or sunflower oil
1 tbs red or white wine vinegar
salt
freshly milled black pepper

Beat the ingredients together in a cup or bowl or shake them vigorously in a jar. The vinaigrette will soon become rich and creamy and should be used immediately. Turn the salad ingredients in the vinaigrette a few times and serve. Never allow fragile salad leaves to linger in the vinaigrette, or they will 'wilt'. On the other hand, robust starchy salads of rice, bread, pasta, beans and lentils should be allowed more time to absorb the flavour of the dressing (see the recipe for *Ensalada de lentejas*).

Balsamic vinaigrette

Proceed as above but substitute extra virgin olive oil and balsamic vinegar; do not beat or shake the mixture vigorously but instead stir gently with a teaspoon. This vinaigrette is sweet and aromatic and is a delicious dressing for more exotic, robust salad leaves, especially bitter red raddichio and chicory (Belgian endive).

Sherry vinaigrette

Similar in character to balsamic vinaigrette, this has the rich, mellow flavour of sherry vinegar and also demands an extra virgin olive oil (you can substitute walnut or hazelnut oil). Make it in the same way and in the same quantities as the balsamic vinaigrette. Use it to dress all manner of leafy salads.

Oriental vinaigrette

This 'vinaigrette' brings a touch of the Far East to a crunchy salad of sliced cucumbers and shredded cos (romaine) lettuce. Put in a bowl: 2 tbs rice vinegar, 2 tbs peanut oil, 2 tsp Chinese sesame oil, 2 tsp dark soy sauce, 1 crushed and chopped garlic clove, 1 tsp sugar, pinch of salt, pinch of cayenne. Mix everything together and set aside for about 15 minutes to allow the garlic to flavour the vinaigrette. Remove the garlic, pour over the salad, mix well and serve.

Chili vinaigrette

The flavours of the 'vinaigrette' are hot, sweet, sour and salty, a combination typical of south-east Asia. Mix together in a bowl: 2 tbs rice vinegar, 1 tbs peanut oil, 2 tsp sugar, 1 tbs Thai fish sauce, 1 thinly sliced spring onion (scallion), 2 washed, seeded and finely chopped fresh chilies, and a handful of chopped fresh coriander (cilantro). Use to dress a salad of finely shredded white cabbage or Chinese leaf cabbage.

Ensalada de Lentejas
· · · · · · · · · ·

The flavour of this rustic Spanish lentil salad
improves after a few hours, so it is a good dish to
prepare up to a day in advance. Serve with thin slices
of Parma ham and pickles or with spicy sausages and
mashed potatoes. This makes enough for six people.

225g/8oz green lentils
1 onion, peeled and finely chopped
$\frac{1}{2}$ a stick (stalk) of celery, finely sliced
small carrot, peeled and finely chopped
2 cloves of garlic, peeled and chopped
water
salt
2 tsp mild paprika
1 tbs sherry vinegar
4 tbs extra virgin olive oil
2 peeled shallots or 4 spring onions (scallions), thinly sliced
handful of fresh parsley, washed and chopped

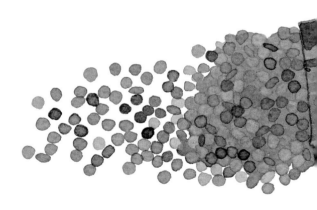

Wash and drain the lentils, then put them in a pot with the onion, celery, carrot and garlic. Cover with water, bring to the boil and simmer with the lid ajar for about 25 minutes or until the lentils are tender.

Drain and transfer to a glass, china or earthenware bowl. While still warm, season with salt and paprika, pour in the sherry vinegar and olive oil, add the shallots or spring onions and the parsley. Mix thoroughly. When cooled, cover and set aside for at least 2 hours.

MEDITERRANEAN COUNTRY SALAD

· · · · · · · · · ·

This is typical of the hearty salads prepared throughout the Mediterranean and other warm European countries, for which the ingredients can be varied according to taste and seasonal availability. It is very good with crusty bread to mop up the juices. This makes enough for two or it will serve four as an appetizer.

110g/4oz white cabbage or Chinese leaf cabbage
110g/4oz lettuce
1 small green pepper
$\frac{1}{2}$ of a cucumber, peeled
225g/8oz tomatoes
1 stick (stalk) of celery
2 spring onions (scallions)
110g/4oz drained canned or cooked fresh corn
110g/4oz boiled green beans
1–2 tbs red wine vinegar
3–4 tbs extra virgin olive oil
salt

Wash the cabbage and lettuce leaves, then blot or shake dry. Shred coarsely and put them in a salad bowl. Remove the cap, pith and seeds of the green pepper and slice the flesh into thin rings. Slice the cucumber, tomatoes, celery and spring onion and add to the bowl together with the corn and green beans.

Beat the vinegar, oil and salt to a creamy consistency, pour over the salad and mix gently but thoroughly. Serve immediately.

Spinach, Bacon and Avocado Salad

. . . .

Use very fresh young spinach and soft, well-ripened avocados which contrast pleasantly with the crisp bacon and the crunchy croûtons. Serves six as a first course.

275g/10oz fresh spinach, washed and patted dry
2 ripe avocados
lemon juice
olive oil, for frying
175g/6oz lean bacon, trimmed and diced
2 cloves of garlic, peeled and crushed
2 slices of bread, cut into small cubes
2 tbs white wine vinegar
5 tbs extra virgin olive oil, walnut oil or hazelnut oil
1 tsp mustard
1 tsp salt

Remove the lower parts of the spinach stalks. Tear the leaves roughly. Peel and stone (pit) the avocados,

cut the flesh into chunks and sprinkle sparingly with lemon juice, turning the chunks so that they are evenly coated.

Heat olive oil in a non-stick frying pan. Fry the bacon until just crisp, then drain on kitchen paper (paper towel). Add the crushed garlic and the bread and fry until the croûtons are golden. Discard the garlic and drain the croûtons on kitchen paper.

Combine all the prepared ingredients in a salad bowl. Beat the vinegar with the extra virgin olive oil or nut oil, mustard and salt until the dressing is creamy. Pour over the salad, mix gently and serve immediately.

Potato Salad

· · · · · · · · · ·

This tasty but relatively light potato salad should be made with small, waxy potatoes that retain their shape and firm texture after boiling. New potatoes are ideal and should be washed thoroughly but left unpeeled. It will keep well in the refrigerator for 12 hours, and serves four people, accompanied by charcuterie and a selection of hors d'oeuvres.

675g/1½ lb small boiling potatoes
4 tbs olive oil
2 tbs white wine vinegar
1 tsp mustard
salt
freshly milled black pepper
110ml/4fl oz/½ cup strained live yoghurt
small bunch of fresh chives, washed and finely chopped

Peel the potatoes if necessary. Boil them until tender, but do not overcook them.

Beat the olive oil with the vinegar, mustard and seasoning. Drain the potatoes well and cut them into chunks unless they are very small. Put them into a bowl.

Stir the dressing again and pour it over the potatoes while they are still hot, turning gently a few times. When they have cooled, fold in the yoghurt. Check the seasoning, add the chives and mix thoroughly. Serve after an hour or so or cover and refrigerate for up to 12 hours.

PICKLING SPICE MIXTURE

Although this recipe does not contain vinegar, it is very useful for pickling and keeps well in a sealed jar. The mixture is highly aromatic, and with its varied subdued colours makes a charming gift when presented in an attractive small container. This makes about 60g/3oz, enough to make 1 litre/1¾ pints of spiced vinegar (see the recipe).

1 tbs cinnamon bark fragments
2 tbs dried sliced ginger or *galangal*
1 tbs allspice berries
1 tbs juniper berries
1 tbs mixed peppercorns
1 tbs coriander seeds
1 tbs green cardamom pods (optional)
2 tsp whole cloves
1 tbs mustard seeds
1 tbs dried chilies
4–6 dried bay leaves, in pieces

Put all the ingredients into a shallow bowl and distribute them evenly. Spoon the mixture into a clean jar, seal tightly and store until required.

SPICED VINEGAR

This vinegar is very handy for making spicy pickles and fruit chutneys. (See the recipes for pickling spices and pickled baby onions.) It is essential to use a bottle with a clean, plastic-lined lid. Alternatively, seal with a clean cork. You can use cider vinegar or white wine vinegar.

3–4 tbs pickling spice mixture
560ml/1 pint/2 cups vinegar

Heat the ingredients in a covered enamelled pan; bring to a gentle simmer, stir, then remove from the heat. Allow the vinegar to cool completely, then strain the liquid into a sterilized glass bottle. Screw on the lid and store in a cool, dark place until required.

PICKLED BABY ONIONS

These pickled onions could not be easier to make, especially if you have a ready-made supply of home-spiced vinegar. These onions go well with bread and cheese and will perk up cold meats and salads. The onions are soaked in a brine solution prior to pickling to soften them and draw out excess moisture.

450g/1lb small pickling onions
water
3 tbs fine or freshly ground sea salt
500ml/⅘ pint/1¾ cups spiced cider or white wine vinegar

Peel the onions, taking care not to break them up.

Put the onions into a pot. Cover with water, add the salt and bring to the boil. Turn off the heat and leave them to soak for about 3 hours. Rinse them thoroughly in fresh water and drain.

Heat the spiced vinegar without boiling. Put the onions into a sterilized pickling jar. Pour in the vinegar, seal and store for 2–3 weeks before opening. Keep in the fridge once opened.

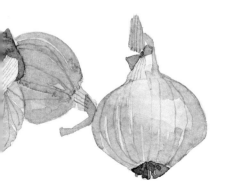

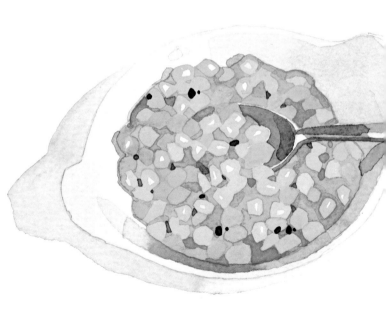

TRADITIONAL CORN RELISH
· · · · · · · · · ·

This is an attractive relish to serve with hamburgers, hot dogs and barbecued steaks. It is best to make it in late summer when fresh corn cobs are cheap, abundant and very good. However, canned or frozen corn kernels may be substituted. This makes about 850ml/1$\frac{1}{2}$ pints of relish.

4 large corn cobs, husked
560ml/1 pint/2 cups water
2–3 tsp salt
1 red pepper
1 large, mild green chili, seeded and chopped
1 onion, peeled and chopped
170ml/6fl oz/$\frac{3}{4}$ cup cider vinegar
4 tbs sugar
3 tbs yellow mustard seeds
1 tbs mustard powder

Boil the corn in enough water to cover, until almost tender. Drain. Sever the kernels from the cobs and transfer to a pot with 560ml/1 pint/2 cups water and the salt.

Remove the cap, pith and seeds of the pepper, then dice the flesh and add to the pot. Add the remaining ingredients. Bring to the boil, reduce the heat to medium-low and cook for about 30 minutes. Put the relish into sterilized glass jars when cool, seal and store in a cool, dark place for about 3 weeks before using. Once opened, keep refrigerated for up to 3 weeks.

PICCALILLI

・・・・・・・・・・

This very traditional English relish will liven up ham, pâtés and other cold meats. It is also very good with bread and cheese. Use spiced vinegar or white wine or cider vinegar warmed just to simmering with about 2 tbs of pickling spice (see the recipes for spiced vinegar and pickling spice). The brine solution draws out some moisture and so prevents the vegetables from diluting the vinegar. It is also important to choose only very fresh, unblemished vegetables. This makes about 1 litre/1³/₄ pints of piccalilli.

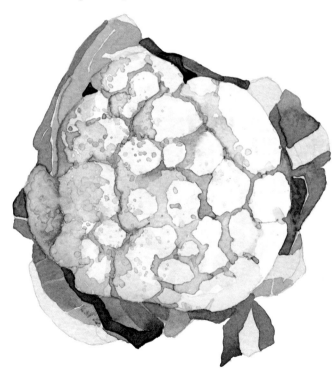

1 medium or $\frac{1}{2}$ of a large cucumber
1 green pepper
1 red pepper
12 pickling onions
$\frac{1}{4}$ of a cauliflower
60g/3oz green beans, topped and tailed
560ml/1 pint/2 cups water
6 tbs ground sea salt
1 tbs mustard powder
1 tbs turmeric powder
560ml/1 pint/2 cups spiced vinegar
3 tbs sugar

Peel and cube the cucumber. Remove the peppers' caps, pith and seeds and dice the flesh. Peel the pickling onions but leave them whole. Cut the cauliflower into small chunks. Slice the green beans into $2\frac{1}{2}$cm/ 1 inch sections.

Bring the water to the boil, adding the salt. Allow to cool. Throw in the vegetables and leave them in the brine solution for 24 hours. (Mix them a few times to ensure that they absorb the brine.) Rinse and drain them well.

In an enamelled pan, make a paste with the mustard, turmeric powder and a little warmed vinegar, stirring constantly. When the paste is smooth, add the rest of the vinegar and the sugar. Mix well, bring to the boil and reduce the volume of liquid approximately by half, stirring frequently. Add the vegetables, mix well and boil for about 10 minutes. Spoon the piccalilli into sterilized jars kept hot in a cool oven, then seal them. When cool, store the jars in a cool, dark place for 3 weeks before opening.

SWEET PEPPER RELISH

. . . .

This relish is best made up about 1 hour before serving. It makes a good accompaniment to grilled (broiled) or barbecued fish, poultry or meat. The quantity below is just enough for four small portions.

1 sweet red pepper
1 sweet yellow pepper
1 sweet orange pepper
(or any combination of the above)
1 large shallot, peeled and thinly sliced
1 tbs red wine vinegar
3 tbs extra virgin olive oil
1 tsp sugar
salt
handful of fresh parsley, washed and finely chopped

Roast the peppers in an oven pre-heated to 200°C/400°F/gas mark 6 until uniformly blackened. Put them in a bowl, cover with a plate and leave to 'steam' for 15 minutes. Slip off and discard the skins. Remove and discard the seeds and white pith, then slice the flesh into thin strips. Put the slices into a shallow bowl and mix in the shallot slices.

Beat the vinegar, oil, sugar, salt and parsley. Pour the mixture over the peppers and set aside for up to 1 hour. Mix well before serving.

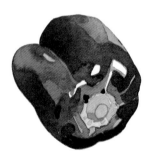

CREMA PICCANTE
· · · · · · · · · · ·

Stir just small amounts of this devilishly hot, wicked-ly tangy pepper sauce into freshly boiled, drained pasta. Dilute 2–3 tbs of *crema* with an equal quantity of the pasta's boiling liquid; this should be sufficient to dress 400g/14oz of *campanelle*, *fusilli* or *penne rigate*, enough for four servings. This recipe makes just under 225ml/8fl oz/1 cup, enough to fill a small, clean jar. Sealed and refrigerated, this should keep for several weeks.

2 sweet red peppers
8–12 medium-hot dried red chilies
2 fresh or canned tomatoes
3 cloves of garlic, peeled
3 tbs red wine vinegar
2 tbs water
generous pinch of oregano
sprig of thyme
3 sprigs of basil
salt
olive oil

Remove the cap, pith and seeds of the peppers. Put the flesh into an enamelled pan together with all the remaining ingredients except for the olive oil. Bring to the boil, cover the pan, reduce the heat and sim-mer for 4 minutes, stirring once or twice to prevent the bottom from burning.

Allow the mixture to cool. Transfer to a food processor and process to a smooth paste, adding 3 tbs olive oil while continuing to blend. When cooled, spoon the *crema* into a sterilized jar, cover with a thin layer of oil and seal tightly. Once opened, use up the sauce within a week.

PICKLED OYSTER MUSHROOMS

Oyster mushrooms are a delicious wild species. They are cultivated successfully and are widely available in supermarkets. (Ordinary mushrooms can also be pickled this way.) The pickling spices counteract much of the tartness of the vinegar, but small portions of these pickled oyster mushrooms make a very good, sharp-tasting hors d'oeuvre served with charcuterie and salads. This recipe makes enough to fill a large pickling jar. If all the equipment is properly sterilized, the mushrooms should keep well for several months.

900g/2lb oyster mushrooms
560ml/1 pint/2 cups white wine vinegar
560ml/1 pint/2 cups water
1 tbs salt
3 bay leaves
6 cloves
1 tsp black peppercorns
1 tsp coriander seeds
1 tsp juniper berries (optional)
1 tsp allspice berries (optional)
3–4 large dried red chilies
olive oil to fill the pickling jar

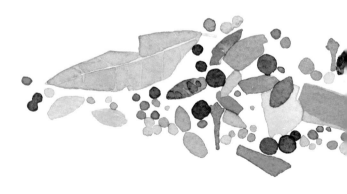

Clean and trim the mushrooms, rejecting any that are bruised or in any way blemished. Slice them or leave them whole, depending upon their size. Put them into a large enamelled pot with all the remaining ingredients except the olive oil. Stir while the liquid comes to the boil.

Cover and simmer for about 8 minutes. Drain, touching the ingredients only with a sterilized spoon (immersed for a few minutes in boiling water), then allow them to cool.

Put the mushrooms and the pickling spices into a sterilized pickling jar. Fill the jar with oil, stirring to release any trapped air bubbles. A generous layer of oil should cover the mushrooms. Seal the jar and store in a cool place for at least a month. Once opened, finish the mushrooms within a month or so; they should keep longer if you use a sterilized fork each time you lift some out.

SPICED RED CABBAGE WITH RAISINS AND APPLES
· · · · · · · · · ·

This is a very popular festive dish in the Scandinavian countries, where it is served with roast goose or the yule ham, adding a frisson of spice to the Christmas table. It may also accompany roast turkey or chicken and makes an excellent vegetarian dish in its own right. Traditionally the cabbage is cooked for about 2 hours, but I prefer to reduce the cooking time to just one hour, which produces very good results. Serves four.

75g/3oz butter
1 large onion, peeled and chopped
900g/2lb red cabbage, shredded
450g/1lb sharp apples, peeled, cored and sliced
3 tbs raisins
110g/4oz/$\frac{1}{2}$ cup brown sugar
pinch of ground cloves
1 tsp ground allspice
1 tsp salt
425ml/$\frac{3}{4}$ pint/1$\frac{1}{2}$ cups red wine
2 tbs wine vinegar
425ml/$\frac{3}{4}$ pint/1$\frac{1}{2}$ cups water

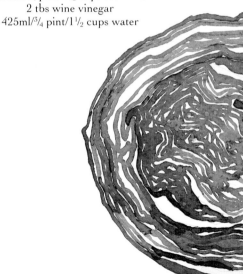

Melt the butter in a large, flameproof casserole and gently cook the onion until lightly browned. Add the cabbage and apples, mix, and cook for a few minutes. Add the remaining ingredients, cover tightly and simmer for 1 hour. Serve hot.

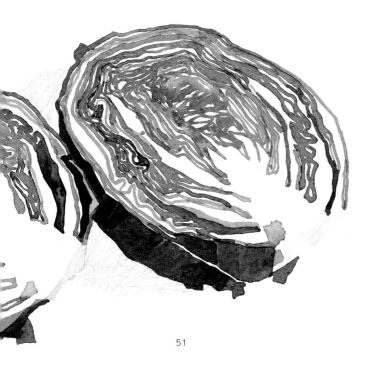

Gravadlax with Mustard Mayonnaise
· · · · · · · · · ·

Gravadlax is very popular in Finland and Sweden where it is traditionally accompanied by boiled potatoes and a tart mustard mayonnaise. I find that the thin slices of tender salmon are just as good sprinkled with wine vinegar or lemon juice and eaten with buttered slices of wholemeal bread. Alternatively, arrange the salmon slices in a fan and serve on small plates next to a little nest of mixed exotic salad leaves, dressed with a generous dollop of mustard mayonnaise. This makes a sophisticated first course that is very suitable for entertaining, since the work must be done in advance. However you choose to serve the gravadlax, the recipes make more than enough for six people.

1kg /2¼lb plump filleted salmon, with the skin on
4 tbs sea salt
freshly milled white or black pepper
4 tbs sugar
small bunch of fresh dill

Wash the salmon fillets, drain, then blot them dry with kitchen paper (paper towel). Sprinkle about 1 tbs salt over the bottom of a dish large enough to accommodate the salmon. Place one salmon fillet on top of the salt, the skin facing down. Sprinkle the flesh with 2 tbs salt, a generous grinding of pepper and half of the sugar. Cover with half of the dill. Place the other fillet on top, the skin facing up. Sprinkle the rest of the salt, pepper, and sugar over the fish, and cover with another layer of dill.

Cover the dish with aluminium foil, top with a plate slightly smaller than the dish and weigh down with a heavy object. Refrigerate for 24–48 hours. Before serving, pour off the liquid that will have collected on the dish, and scrape off the dill and the seasoning. With a sharp knife, slice the fillets thinly, cutting obliquely down to the skin.

Mustard mayonnaise
1 tbs smooth mustard
1 tbs sugar
1 tbs white wine vinegar
salt
freshly milled black pepper
1 egg yolk, at room temperature
6 tbs light vegetable oil

In a food processor, blend the mustard, sugar, vinegar, seasonings and egg yolk, adding the oil in a thin stream with the motor running. Stop as soon as the mayonnaise is thick and glossy and spoon into a serving bowl.

Fish and Chips with Béarnaise Sauce

Although fish and chips are traditionally served wrapped in newspaper, liberally doused with lashings of malt vinegar, and quickly gobbled up with the fingers, they make a splendid lunch or supper dish, accompanied by a good home-made Béarnaise sauce. The vinegar in the Béarnaise does not overwhelm the sweet, delicate flavour of fresh cod or haddock. This Béarnaise can be made in advance and kept refrigerated for up to 48 hours. (Traditionalists may prefer to ignore this recommendation and stick to their malt vinegar!) Serves two.

Easy Béarnaise
110g/4oz/¼ cup butter
2 tbs white wine vinegar
4 tbs white wine
½ tsp coarsely ground black pepper
1 shallot, peeled and finely chopped
2 egg yolks, at room temperature
pinch of salt
pinch of cayenne
chopped fresh tarragon
chopped chervil or parsley

Melt the butter in a small pan. Let it cool slightly but do not allow it to solidify.

In an enamelled pan reduce the vinegar and wine together with the black pepper and shallot to about 1 tbs of liquid. Let the contents of the pan cool slightly; they should be warm.

Put the pan contents, the egg yolks, salt, cayenne and a dribble of melted butter into the bowl of a food processor and process briefly. With the motor running, add the melted butter little by little. Mix in the herbs when the sauce has the consistency of custard and use immediately or put into a covered container and refrigerate (warm before serving).

Fish and chips

The secrets of good fish and chips are as follows: make a light batter with an equal quantity of flour and very cold water, choose very fresh fillets of cod or haddock, and use only floury potatoes with a high starch content. (Immersion in very hot oil for the first few minutes seals the potatoes, which should then be removed from the fat, rested in a colander and returned for a second fry, a procedure that makes them light and crisp.)

peanut and olive oil, for frying
575g/1¼ lb floury potatoes, peeled and 'chipped'
110g/4oz/½ cup plain (all-purpose) flour
110ml/4fl oz/½ cup cold water
salt
2 cod or haddock fillets
1 lemon, quartered

Heat a generous layer of peanut and olive oil in a very large, non-stick frying pan. When smoking, add the potatoes. Remove them after 3 minutes and drain in a colander. Turn off the heat.

Mix the flour, water and a good pinch of salt very thoroughly, ensuring that no lumps remain. Heat a similarly generous volume of oil in a fresh non-stick pan. While it heats to smoking point, dip the fish fillets in the batter to give an even coating. Slip them into the oil just as it starts to smoke, turning the fish carefully after 3 minutes.

Meanwhile, re-heat the other pan, and when the oil is hot, return the partly cooked potatoes. They will be ready in about 3 minutes, unless very thickly cut, to coincide with the fish which should be cooked golden-brown on the outside with a white, moist interior. Drain the potatoes and the fish on kitchen paper (paper towel) and serve quickly on warmed plates, garnished with lemon quarters and with a generous helping of Béarnaise sauce.

SOFRITO

· · · · · · · · · ·

These delicious braised steaks are a speciality of Corfu and the beautiful wooded island of Paxos, which lies just a few miles to the south of Corfu. *Sofrito* was probably introduced to the region by the Venetians, hence the Italianate name. You will need a tender cut of beef or veal and an aged red wine or sherry vinegar. Making enough for four, in island tavernas this is invariably served with the ubiquitous French fries, although puréed potatoes are a better accompaniment.

1kg/2¼ lb thin sirloin steaks, trimmed of fat
salt
freshly milled black pepper
flour, to coat the steaks
6 tbs olive oil
4 cloves of garlic, peeled and sliced
1 ripe tomato, peeled and chopped
3 tbs red wine or sherry vinegar
110ml/4fl oz/½ cup red wine
small handful of fresh mint, washed and chopped

Place the steaks between sheets of plastic or greaseproof (waxed) paper and beat them a few times with a mallet or a rolling pin, to flatten them.

Season both sides and dip them in flour. Heat the olive oil in a large, well-seasoned or non-stick frying pan. Fry the steaks until both sides are lightly browned (you may need to do this in two batches). Return the first batch of steaks to the pan, add the remaining ingredients, mix well and cook over a medium heat until the sauce is thick and the oil has begun to separate (6–8 minutes). Serve immediately.

BURDETTO
· · · · · · · · · ·

This pungent fish stew is a legacy of the Venetian occupation of the Greek island of Corfu. *Burdetto* is related to the many thick fish soups – called *brodetti* – of Italy's Adriatic coast. In Corfu, scorpion fish is generally used, but any firm, white-fleshed but assertively flavoured fish such as red mullet will produce good results. The fish may be kept whole, cut into pieces or filleted. Serves four.

110ml/4fl oz/$\frac{1}{2}$ cup olive oil
1 onion, peeled and chopped
3 cloves of garlic, peeled and chopped
2 tbs hot paprika (or 2 tbs mild paprika and
$\frac{1}{2}$ tsp cayenne)
salt
450g/1lb ripe peeled tomatoes or canned tomatoes,
chopped
2 tbs red wine vinegar
1kg/2$\frac{1}{4}$lb fish, cleaned and scaled
(or 900g/2lb filleted fish)
small handful of fresh parsley, washed and chopped

Pre-heat the oven to 200°C/400°F/gas mark 6.

Heat the olive oil and sauté the onion until soft. Add the garlic, paprika (and cayenne, if using) and simmer for a few minutes. Season, add the tomatoes and vinegar and simmer the sauce until it has thickened slightly (about 15 minutes).

Place the fish in a large oven dish, spoon over the sauce and cover the dish. Bake for 15–20 minutes, depending upon whether the fish are in pieces or whole. The oil should have started to separate from the sauce and the fish should be cooked through. Garnish with parsley and serve immediately, accompanied by sautéed potatoes or French fries.

STIFADHO
· · · · · · · · · ·

Vinegar and cinnamon are both ubiquitous flavouring ingredients in Greek kitchens; together with tiny whole pickling onions, they give this popular and meltingly tender beef stew its authentically tart and spicy character. This serves four, accompanied by pasta or potatoes.

900g/2lb good braising steak, trimmed of fat
110ml/4fl oz/¹/₂ cup olive oil
900g/2lb small pickling onions, peeled
4 cloves of garlic, peeled and chopped
small piece of celery, with leaves attached
2 tbs tomato purée (paste)
425ml/³/₄ pint/1¹/₂ cups water
2cm/1 inch piece of cinnamon bark
salt
freshly milled black pepper
3 tbs good wine vinegar

Cut the beef into large, even cubes, each about 4cm/1³/₄ inches in size.

Heat the olive oil in a large, lidded casserole and brown the beef. Remove it and lightly brown the onions. Remove and reserve them.

Return the beef and its juices to the casserole, add the garlic, celery, tomato purée, water, and cinnamon. Season, mix and bring back to the boil. Cover the pan, lower the heat and simmer very gently for 1 hour. Return the onions to the casserole and continue to simmer for a further 45 minutes.

About 10 minutes before serving, turn off the heat and stir in the vinegar. Serve hot.

AROMATIC BARBECUED CHICKEN BREASTS

· · · · · · · · · ·

This powerful herbal marinade really penetrates the chicken breasts, and the balsamic vinegar sweetens and tenderizes the flesh. For best results, barbecue the chicken breasts over charcoal, although they may also be grilled (broiled) conventionally. Accompany with rice and a salad. Serves four.

4 corn-fed or free-range chicken breasts, skins intact
salt

Marinade
2 cloves of garlic, crushed
4 tbs balsamic vinegar
4 tbs olive oil
salt
1 tsp black peppercorns
2 bay leaves
sprig of parsley
sprig of thyme
sprig of rosemary
sprig of sage

Prick the chicken breasts all over with the point of a sharp knife and put them into a china or glass bowl. Do not add the salt at this stage.

Add the marinade ingredients, mix well and tuck the fresh herbs under the chicken breasts. Cover the bowl and refrigerate for 12–24 hours, turning the chicken breasts a few times to distribute the marinade evenly.

Lift the chicken breasts from the marinade and barbecue or grill for 10–15 minutes, or until the skins are slightly charred and the centres are white. (Baste each one once with a little marinade.) Sprinkle with a little salt just before serving.

MARINATED CHICKEN BREASTS WITH SUN-DRIED TOMATO RELISH
· · · · · · · · · ·

I created this recipe to demonstrate how ingredients that are typically found in Mediterranean kitchens can be cooked superbly according to Oriental techniques. As Marcella Hazan and others have observed before, Italian and Chinese cooking occasionally bear an uncannily close resemblance. This quick and delicious dish serves two.

2 corn-fed or free-range chicken breasts, skins removed
2 tbs olive oil, for stir-frying
splash of white wine

Marinade
2 tbs extra virgin olive oil
2 tbs sherry vinegar
2 cloves of garlic, peeled and crushed

Sun-dried tomato relish
5 marinated sun-dried tomato halves, from a jar
1 tbs pine nuts (pine kernels)
½ of a clove of garlic, peeled
½ of a dried red chili
pinch of salt
1 tsp wine vinegar
3 tbs extra virgin olive oil

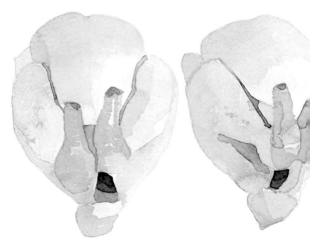

Slice the chicken breasts diagonally into strips about 2½cm/1 inch wide. Pierce them repeatedly with the point of a sharp knife and put them into a bowl. Add the remaining marinade ingredients, turn the chicken in the mixture a few times, cover the bowl and set aside for at least 2 hours.

Blend the relish ingredients to a paste in a food processor, or pound them with a mortar and pestle. Divide into 2 portions.

Lift the chicken strips from the marinade, discarding the garlic. Heat a wok until it smokes. Pour in the olive oil and quickly add the chicken strips. Stir-fry for 3 minutes, then splash in a little wine. Continue to stir-fry for 2 more minutes, taking care not to burn the chicken; very little liquid should remain.

Serve the chicken and the relish at once on warmed plates, accompanied by rice or mashed potatoes and a green salad.

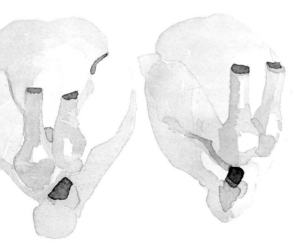

Sweet and Sour Chicken

. . . .

Once you have cooked this delicious, authentic and very easy Chinese recipe you will never again tolerate tired, soggy, sweet and sour pork. As the chicken is stir-fried with several vegetables – you could also add some sliced water chestnuts or bamboo shoots – plain boiled rice is the only necessary accompaniment. Serves two.

2 corn-fed or free-range chicken breasts, skins removed
110g/4oz fresh pineapple, peeled
1 large carrot, scrubbed
1 green pepper
3 spring onions (scallions), washed
1 tbs sugar
3 tbs rice vinegar
4 tbs water
1 tbs tomato ketchup
2 tbs light soy sauce
1 tsp flour
2 tbs water
3 tbs peanut oil
2 cloves of garlic, peeled and sliced
2 tbs Shaohsing wine or dry sherry

Cut the chicken breasts into 2cm/1¼ inch cubes. Cut the pineapple into small chunks. Slice the carrot obliquely into very thin oval discs. Remove the cap, pith and seeds of the green pepper and dice the flesh. Cut the spring onions into 1½cm/½ inch sections, setting aside the green ones.

Dissolve the sugar in the vinegar, water, ketchup and soy sauce, stirring thoroughly. Set aside. Dissolve the flour in the water and set aside.

Heat the oil in a wok. Add the chicken, toss in the oil a few times, then add the garlic and stir-fry for 1 minute. Add the Shaohsing wine or sherry, stir, then put in the pineapple chunks and all the other vegetables except for the green spring onion. Toss for 30 seconds. Pour in the sweet and sour sauce and the flour mixture and continue to stir until the liquid has thickened (about 3 more minutes). Sprinkle with the green spring onion sections and serve at once.

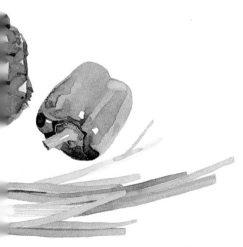